EZ

Steps to Creating
a Great Logo

The Comprehensive Guide to Creating a Timeless Logo

Joseph Thompson

DEDICATION

I would like to dedicate this book to my mother Eve thank you for you love and encouragement and to my sister Deborah Thompson thanks for always pushing me to be a man of integrity.

CONTENTS

ACKNOWLEDGMENTS

I would like to acknowledge all the nice folks at the New York City public library for the help and use of their facilities in order to complete my work.

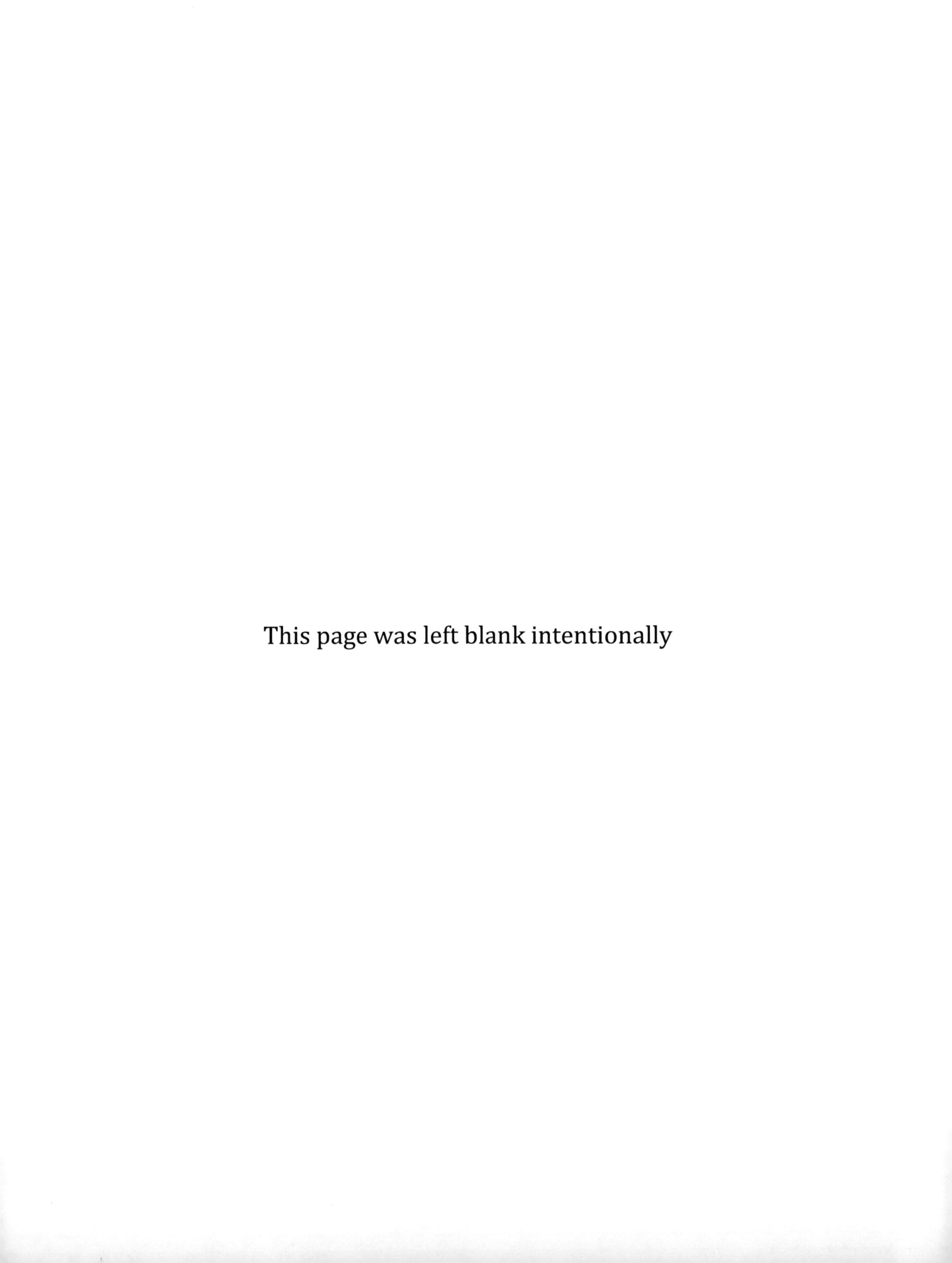

This page was left blank intentionally

Chapter 1

What is a logo exactly?

A logo should symbolize everything a company is about from what products it is offering for sale to it positioning and personality and key message; this need to be represented by the logo's typeface, shape and style as well as colors. A logo doesn't always have to look or say exactly what it is that a business does for example, take the fast food chain Popeye's Chicken its company's logo is represented by the letter P in a circle an d the words Popeye's next to it. I know what you are thinking when you hear the word Popeye you are thinking of the cartoon character of a sailor who gain super strength from eating his spinach but no this Popeye's sells fried chicken so as you can see the logo can be far removed from the product you offer but it is quiet ingenious because we all love Popeye. So in this case the logo designer created a timeless logo and a psychologically strong subliminal message in the customers mind.

Steps to follow in order to great a great looking Logo

The first step in creating a great looking logo is to be unique you can be the first to experiment a concept by breaking some of the rules. Because if you copy your competitors logo or a popular brand you run the risk of not being recognized as a different company and small or no market share. Secondly, trends come and go so don't follow the crowd or in this case the trend instead try to create a logo that will stand the test of time so in the long run you would not have to recreate your brand. Most importantly it should also be the right fit for your business. Third, if you follow this golden rule (Keep it Simple Stupid) K.I.S.S all the great logos are the ones that seem to be the simplest; so if you keep it simple and don't overdo it you will be on the right track. Take logos like Apple, Sears, Visa or MasterCard they are very simple but are timeless. In addition, be transparent always try to think about what you want to achieve with your logo and the message it is going to send both versions you have online on your website and printed versions because it is very important when considering to create your own brand. Lastly, it helps to know and keep the companies goals in mind when creating your brand. This will help you not to get off track.

Chapter 2

Geometric Shapes in Logos

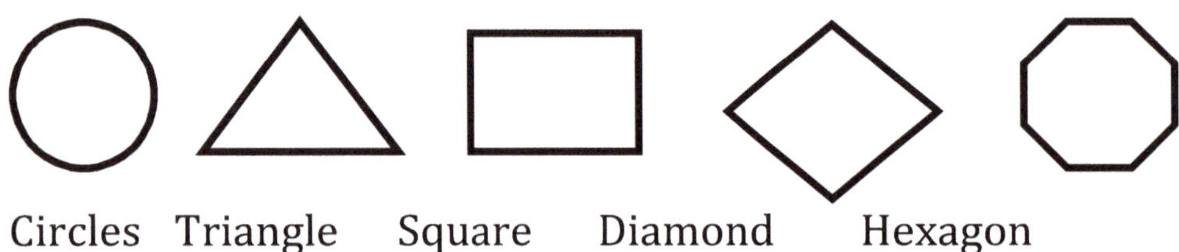

Circles   Triangle   Square   Diamond   Hexagon

Circles

Using circles in your logo can be interrupted in many different ways due to the cultural differences but we can all agree on some universal meanings Circles can protect, they also keep things within, they also have no beginning or no end, it even suggest community and integrity, circles are also warm, they can even suggest power and energy unity and infinite as well as harmony. Quite a few companies use circles in there logo such as Target, Audi, Audi and many more.

Triangles

Triangles can be stable and are known to have energy and power they are also balanced an can be found in companies dealing with law, science and religion it even suggests self-discovery, revelation, purpose, progression masculinity and direction.

Squares and Rectangles

Rectangles have right angles an can suggest order rationality, formality this is the most common shaped used in many companies logos throughout the modern free world. This shape also suggests honesty and are seen as earthbound, it is can also mean conformity, peacefulness solidity security and equality. Many companies such as Microsoft has embraced this shape in its companies branding guidelines even Siemens the global engineer firm has also use this shape it is very popular among the business community.

Colors in Logos

Color is one of the most identifiable aspects of creating brand identity. Using colors correctly is one of the easiest ways to make sure materials reflect a cohesive brand.

So the more robust the color palette will provide many design options. However, restraint must be considered to make sure you don't lose your brands identity.

Combining colors and shapes can give a logo dynamic effect colors like red, blue, orange, purple, gold, black and white are very popular colors, and are used in a lot of major brand logos they also have deep psychological meaning and could affect how your customers feel about your brand.

ORANGE Symbolizes enthusiasm, fascination, joy, creativity, determination, attraction, achievement, encouragement

RED

Symbolizes Anger, Passion, Excitement, Death, Health, Love

Chapter 4

BLUE

Symbolizes Trust, Authority, Powers, Professionalism, Loyalty, Benevolence

GREEN

Symbolizes Harmony, Natural, Caring, Plentiful, Nature, Peace

YELLOW

Symbolizes Happiness, Warmth, Caution, Relaxation, Positivity, Alter Mood

Chapter 5

GREY

Symbolizes: Neutral, Balanced color, Emotionless, Formal, Conservative, Sadness Isolation

BLACK

Symbolizes: Authority, Power, Mystery, Boldness, Elegance, Sophistication, Mystery

Chapter 6

Now let us create a logo for a fictitious company by the name of **American Yard Boys**, let us say they sell apparel jeans to be exact now here are a few way you can go about setting up the logo first you think of the brand and who the company will be targeting so that you design concept don't appeal to the wrong target market

Step 1. Select your colors

Step 2. Choose a Font

Font Family: Cooperplate Gothic
Select a font that fits your brand

Step 3. Select a rectangle

Step 4. Add a fill color to your rectangle

Step 5. Add Your Brand Name

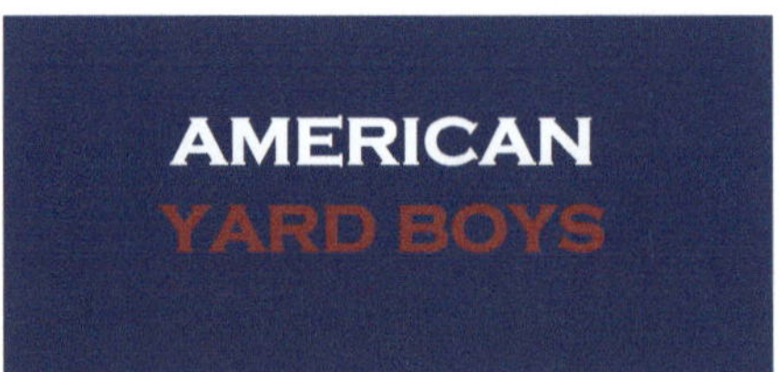

Step 6. If you wanted to add some extra like a symbol you can do that or you can add a gradient or pattern to your background it all depends on the message and your target market you want to appeal to and the look and feel you want your brand to have

Now when you create your logo do not forget to group your shapes and text in order to form the new shape or logo you have just created and saving your logo is very important you can save different version of you logo for example PNG, JPEG,TIFF,PDF, EPS, AI, PSD file it all depends on the software you are using to create your logo.

NEXT LEVEL
BARBERSHOP

NEXT LEVEL
BARBERSHOP

NEXT LEVEL
BARBERSHOP

NEXT LEVEL
BARBERSHOP

NEXT LEVEL
BARBERSHOP

NEXT
LEVEL
BARBERSHOP

NEXT LEVEL
BARBERSHOP

NEXT LEVEL
BARBERSHOP

NEXT LEVEL
BARBERSHOP

Rosalie Dance School

Rosalie Dance School

Rosalie Dance School

Rosalie Dance School

Rosalie Dance School

Rosalie Dance School

Rosalie Dance School

CHARISE'S
BEAUTY SHOP

Charise's Beauty Shop
Senior Stylist & Great Lengths Extensions Expert

Charise's Beauty Shop
Senior Stylist & Great Lengths Extensions Expert

Charise's Beauty Shop
Senior Stylist & Great Lengths Extensions

CHARISE'S BEAUTY SHOP
Senior Stylist & Great Lengths Extensions

Charise's Beauty Shop
Senior Stylist & Great Lengths
Extensions Expert

Charise's Beauty Shop
Senior Stylist & Great Lengths
Extensions Expert

Charise's Beauty Shop
Senior Stylist & Great Lengths
Extensions Expert

Charise's Beauty Shop
Senior Stylist & Great Lengths
Extensions Expert

Charise's Beauty Shop
Senior Stylist & Great Lengths
Extensions Expert

Charise's Beauty Shop
Senior Stylist & Great Lengths
Extensions Expert

Charise's Beauty Shop
Senior Stylist & Great Lengths Extensions Expert

Ventura's Landscaping

Ventura's Landscaping

Ventura's Landscaping

Ventura's
Landscaping

Ventura's
Landscaping

Ventura's
LANDSCAPING

Ventura's
Landscaping

Ventura's Landscaping

Ventura's
Landscaping

Ventura's
Landscaping

VENTURA'S
LANDSCAPING

Ventura's Landscaping

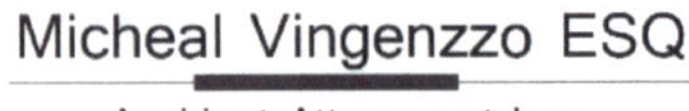

BALLERS
WINTER LEAGUE
YONKERS, NEW YORK TRYOUTS
BALLERS
BALLERS
YONKERS TRYOUTS
BALLERS
BALLERS

J
John's Plumbing Service
SERVING THE ENTIRE PLANET

John's Plumbing Service
SERVING THE ENTIRE PLANET

JOHN'S PLUMBING SERVICE
SERVING THE ENTIRE PLANET

John's
Plumbing Service

J
JOHN'S PLUMBING SERVICE
SERVING THE ENTIRE PLANET

JOHN'S PLUMBING SERVICE
SERVING THE ENTIRE PLANET

John's Plumbing Service
SERVING THE ENTIRE PLANET

John's
Plumbing Service

JOHN'S PLUMBING SERVICE
SERVING THE ENTIRE

John's Plumbing Service
SERVING THE ENTIRE PLANET

John's Plumbing Service
SERVING THE ENTIRE PLANET

John's Plumbing Service
SERVING THE ENTIRE PLANET

PATTY & JIM'S DINER
We are open 24 hours

Patty & Jim's Diner
We are open 24 hours

PJ's
Patty & Jim's Diner
We are open 24 hours

Patty & Jim's Diner
We are open 24 hours

P
Patty & Jim's Diner
We are open 24 hours

P
Patty & Jim's
We are open 24 hours

PJs
Patty & Jim's Diner
We are open 24 hours

Patty & Jim's Diner
We are open 24 hours

Patty & Jim's
Diner
We are open 24 hours

Patty & Jims
Diner
We are open 24 hours

Patty & Jim's Diner
We are open 24

Patty & Jim's Diner
We are open 24 hours

ALIVE
NEWS
3
NEW YORK

3
ALIVE
NEWS
NEW YORK

3
ALIVE
NEWS
NEW YORK

ALIVE
3
NEWS

3
ALIVE
NEWS

ALIVE
NEWS
3
NEW YORK

ALIVE
NEWS

ALIVE
NEWS LEADERS
3

ALIVE
NEWS

ALIVE NEWS
3

OG
DESIGN COMPANY

ORIONGRAPHICS

ORION GRAPHICS

ORION
GRAPHICS

TM

ORION GRAPHICS
DESIGN COMPANY

ORIONGRAPHICS
DESIGN COMPANY

ORION
GRAPHIC DESIGN COMPANY